Prof. S. Willard
from the Author

From the "Burnham Book Store"
Oct. 95 $ .35

MR. BENJAMIN'S POEM,

SPOKEN BEFORE THE

ALUMNI OF WASHINGTON COLLEGE.

A POEM

ON

THE MEDITATION OF NATURE,

SPOKEN

SEPTEMBER 26TH, 1832,

BEFORE THE ASSOCIATION OF THE

ALUMNI OF WASHINGTON COLLEGE.

BY PARK BENJAMIN.

HARTFORD:
PUBLISHED BY F. J. HUNTINGTON.

1832.

TO

THE MEMBERS

OF

THE ASSOCIATION

OF THE

ALUMNI OF WASHINGTON COLLEGE,

The following Poem,

SPOKEN AT THEIR FIRST PUBLIC MEETING,

IS AFFECTIONATELY INSCRIBED.

PREFACE.

Some apology is due to the public for this appearance of a poem which was intended only for the ears of an indulgent audience. The urgent solicitation of friends has become a threadbare excuse—still, it must now be offered. The author takes praise to himself for having, upon former occasions, resisted with fortitude such solicitation ; and if, in yielding in the present instance, to the expressed wishes of several gentlemen of learning and taste, he acts unwisely, he has in reserve the sweet consolation of blaming his advisers.

The author might have chosen, for his poetical essay, a subject more original ; but when he came to reflect that he was to address an assembly composed chiefly of young men, who had been graduated from College but five years at farthest, he made choice of a theme which could not fail to be pleasing to them, both from the facility with which it could be comprehended and from its harmonious association with all their brightest conceptions of the sublime and beautiful. He must soar boldly and loftily and on a vigorous pinion, who, in so short a time, would pass in imagination above the scenes of the glorious creation of God. Yet if, in witnessing this humble flight, one mind can be made to feel the exalting and purifying influences of those works, which millions of spiritual creatures with ceaseless praise behold both day and night, excellent and entire will be the reward of

THE AUTHOR.

THE MEDITATION OF NATURE.

HOW priceless is the lesson that we learn
  From Nature's bright, yet ever-varying, page!
In youth's warm glow, when rays of promise burn,
  And in the frosty evening of old age,
One joy abides within the fervent heart,
Which only can with life and hope depart.
It is to gaze on Nature, and to feel,
Though time may on our pathway darkly steal
And veil the firmament with gathering shades,
That her surpassing beauty never fades;
That slow decay can never waste her forms
  Of stirring grandeur or serene repose:—
Around her sweep the lightning-pinioned storms,
  Upon her bosom rest the glittering snows,
Still she revives, and, undecaying, smiles;
  Her waters leap in gladness to the sea,
Brighter than emeralds gleam her myriad isles,
  Along her shores, the soft gale wafted free,

O'er the vast continent careering, flings
Odor and freshness from its balmy wings!
Hence in youth's vigor and defenceless age,
We read this lesson on her lustrous page;—
'The spirit that pervades us cannot die;
The form it animates may coldly lie
In the dark dwelling-place from whence it came;
The soul shall live eternally the same!'
Life cannot pass away—the vernal bloom
Will spread its beauty even o'er a tomb;
The tree, once riven by the crushing storm,
In greener robes may clothe its stately form;
The stream, released from Winter's icy chain,
Will flash more joyously in Spring's mild reign;
And purer, clearer, seems the light that flows
Where parted clouds the stainless heaven disclose—
So, when this dull humanity decays,
Bright and immortal is the spirit's blaze.
This truth celestial will forever shine,
  To gild the waves of life's uncertain sea,
An emanation from the source divine
  Where glory dwells—the shrine of Deity.
Illumining creation, it will cheer
  Our young, unsullied morning, with its light,
And, when the shadows of past years appear,
  Extend along the dim, approaching night.

Distrust and doubt and fear will never spread
  Their ill-foreboding shadows, to conceal
The ray that time will on existence shed,
  If, in the lesson Nature will reveal
To such as love her truly, we can find
Some glorious emblems of the deathless mind.

Brothers, we meet, perchance, to part forever!
  And now, while on this narrow verge we stand,
Where hand from hand and heart from heart must sever,
  And link from link of friendship's golden band
Must fall apart to be entwined no more,
  I strike the chords of my unheeded lyre;
And though it breathe no song of classic lore,
  Nor glow with inspiration's hidden fire,
Nor warble, like the shell of that strange child
Who with sweet tones the listening gods beguiled;
Yet, turning o'er in memory's treasure-cell
Clear gems of thought beloved and hoarded well,
I feel the lustre of their holy light
Shed through my soul a beam serenely bright;
And if within your hearts I wake one tone,
Whose music is responsive to my own,
Or call up visions of departed hours
To bloom and blush, like Eden's fadeless flowers,
Or cause some moments of this autumn day

On fleeter pinion to be borne away;
Then will the Muse, who taught his fervent strain,
Deem that her votary has not sung in vain.

Of Nature's pure philosophy I sing:—
And my entire devotion and the flame
Of quenchless love upon her altar fling;
For she has ever been to me the same
Unchanging parent, generous and kind;
And all its better nourishment my mind
Draws from her bosom, and my heart would be
Cold as an iceberg of the northern sea,
If, when I gaze on her undying forms,
I did not speak the gratitude which warms
The flowing water of its deepest fountains.
Her quiet vales and her majestic mountains,
Her angry seas, that struggle with the wrath
Of the fierce tempest, rushing from the sky
To rend the earth in his destructive path,
Or flash revenge from his dark shrouded eye,—
Her still lakes, sleeping in the starlight beams,
Her warring cataracts, her peaceful streams,
The boundless prairie where the eagle soars,
The solemn grandeur of her ancient woods,
The haggard rocks that guard her bending shores,
Her green retreats and leafy solitudes,

All fill my soul with reverential awe ;
For everywhere I read the changeless law
That tells its immortality and learn
  Lessons of wisdom, purer than the deep
And strangely-wrought philosophies, that burn
  And waste the spirit, when subduing sleep
Should lull the wearied senses, and the brain
Form golden visions to relieve the pain
Of ceaseless thought, which, ere youth's roses bloom,
Oft strews their blossoms on an early tomb.

Of all your number, brothers, few have passed
Into the prime of manhood—few have cast
On life's broad sea your pennons to the air ;
  Time has not shed from his swift-gliding plume
A silver token 'mid your unthinned hair,
  Or stolen from your cheeks their pleasant bloom ;
And therefore I would seal this glowing truth
  Upon your hearts, before the world has chilled
The earnest fervor of unfettered youth,
  Or busy scenes their noble action stilled.
While you can read on Nature's varied page,
In your best strength or tottering old age,
The soul's high destiny—the unconfined
And soaring freedom of the immortal mind,
While you can learn from every tree and flower

Some moral, to improve the passing hour,
And while you feel that each created thing
Some valued lesson to the heart can bring ;
Then while these mortal temples shall endure,
The flames that light them will be bright and pure.
But when upon that outspread page you see
No sunbright types of immortality,
When tree and flower and wood and stream and vale
To wake to life your fairer virtues fail,
And, over mount and sea and through the sky
Imagination can no longer fly
To bathe its pinions in celestial air—
Then, only then, with saddened thought, despair ;
For, like the rose that blossomed yesterday,
Your feeling's freshness has been thrown away.
Oh then, if we would keep undimm'd the young
  And dear affections of our better years,
When Hope, mild angel, on our pathway flung
  Beams to dispel the mist of darkening fears,
Let us go forth and hold communion sweet
  With the invisible spirit that surrounds
Earth's silent altars—let us go forth to greet
  The woven strain of most enchanting sounds
That stir the clear waves of the golden air ;
Let us go forth and mutely worship there !
From life's unvarying round, oh let us steal

Some fleeting moments we may call our own,
When, unrestrained, the heart can deeply feel
The quiet happiness to be alone.
Alone with Nature in some voiceless glen,
Or by some forest brook, or on the height
Of some uprising hill—away from men,
The city's busy tumult and the sight
Of all the sons of pleasure and of pain,
Where the free soul must feel its human chain.
Then, if within our hearts reflected lie
The perfect glories of the earth and sky,
If every feeling they inspire be fraught
With the pure essence of exalted thought,
Well may we deem, that round each bosom's throne
Float the white robes of Innocence alone!
The man, who cannot see the light divine
Which circles round creation's altar-shrine,
Can, through his tuneless spirit, never feel
The magic sweetness of her spirit steal.
For him, intent on small, corroding cares,
No sunny smile the face of Nature wears.
The grateful verdure of the cooling shade,
That shields the fixed and burning heat of noon,
Sweet Evening's blushes as they softly fade,
The mild, undying beauty of the moon,
Convey to him no blessing—the free waves

That leap and sparkle in the mellow light,
The groves of coral and the gem-hung caves,
Clothed with the horror of the deep midnight,
And all the calm sublimity that dwells
On mountain tops or in untrodden dells,
And loftiest scenes of grandeur can control
No deep emotion of his rayless soul.
And though upon the sapphire arch above,
Glowed the bright beacons of eternal love,
Vain, vain would be your ardent search to find
One starbeam mirrored on his guilty mind.
God grant, my brothers, that in after years
You still may gaze, with undiminished joy,
On all that now so glorious appears,
While life's pure gold is dim with no alloy,
And Feeling strews her wreaths of simple flowers
Upon the track of your unfaded hours.
Oh, let us cherish, with a miser's care,
Our love of all that 's beautiful and fair
In the bright world before us—let us learn
How clear the fountains of instruction flow
From Nature's free and unexhausted urn;
And from the toil of study let us go
To read her priceless lessons, and to view
Upon Heaven's distant realms of trackless blue,

On the broad ocean, or the extended land,
The glowing impress of one mighty hand.

Gaze on the sun in his imperial height!
  Beneath his eye uncounted planets lay,
Wide o'er creation pours his lavish light,
  From the beginning he has ruled the day.
How kingly is his sceptre! see him wave
  Its lustre o'er the firmament—and where
Fly the wild tempests that beneath him rave?
  No trace of storm-cloud lingers on the air;
But Heaven is beauteous as the pensive smile,
  When joy succeeds to sorrow in the heart.
And oh, how brightly gleams that crimson smile,
  Eve's lonely star, serenely and apart,
When o'er the east the rainbow's arch is thrown,
And sinks the day-god, gorgeous and alone!
There's glory in his setting—but the time,
When, like a monarch from his throne sublime,
He gazes o'er the world in mightiest power,
Comes with the stillness of the morning hour.
On all alike his equal radiance streams;
The humblest flower receives his earliest beams,
The smallest fountain revels in his ray,
Beneath his glance old Ocean's billows play,
His smiles upon the lowliest valley rest,

And proudly glisten on the mountain's crest,
He looks as sweetly on the cottage home
As on the splendor of a regal dome,
And each faint star, that gems the distant sky,
Drinks the full lustre of his glorious eye!

Oh, when to rest the wearied day retires,
How, on God's temple, burn the unwasting fires!
Pure, soft and still, each in its own blue sphere,
  As when at first the mighty Maker framed
The bending arch and bade its gleams appear
Where the great sun had through the ether flamed.
Forever beautiful! forever bright!
  What is your hidden mystery? do ye stream
From the clear fountains of celestial light,
  And each to earth display a broken gleam
Of Heaven's immortal glory? are ye strewn
  Along the borders of that fadeless shore,
Which lies beyond those depths unseen, unknown,
  To light the course of angel-plumes, that soar
High through your rainbow-coloured atmosphere?
  Or are ye brilliant melodies—embodied forms
Of thrilling sound made so divinely clear—
  Bright tones from lips that inspiration warms?
Or, as such perfect loveliness ye fling,
  With hope and joy the spirit to inspire,

Are ye not glimpses of those chords that string,
 In glittering order, Heaven's melodious lyre ?
The mystery cannot be known of those bright stars,
 Till the free soul, above the realm of night,
Can view the journeying of their silvery cars ;
 Yet, in the hour of their unwavering light,
Oh, look upon their purity and seek
The shadowed path of Nature—it will speak,
In mildest cadence, a celestial spell
To guard your holiest affections well.

But should imagination droop and fail,
 While soaring thus through regions pure and high ;
And, like an eagle, when the hurrying gale
 Heaves the dark turrets of a clouded sky—
On faultering pinion seek some place of rest,
Then turn and gaze upon the glittering crest
Of the broad ocean, or behold the grand
And beaming features of your own green land !
On the free waters let your vision dwell ;
 See how they flash beneath the golden ray !
Hark, how they murmur—as their surging swell
 Breaks at your feet and slowly rolls away !
Like nodding plumes and helms and glistening spears,
 The serried waves come rushing o'er the main ;
Then, like a host, subdued by sudden fears,

They scatter brokenly to charge again!
Where the horizon meets the glimmering sea,
What fragile mists are floating! Look, once more—
A sail! a sail! and yet it cannot be—
'Tis but a sea-bird that doth lightly soar;
And where yon billows, like strewn diamonds, gleam,
I soon shall hear his shrill, rejoicing scream!
And can such radiant beauty ever wear
The shadow of the tempest? Will its proud
And vengeful rider, in deep midnight, tear
The folded blackness of the thunder-cloud,
Unchain his lightnings and arouse these waves,
Which now are whispering to the peaceful deep
Or calmly resting in their hidden caves,
To leap like lions startled from their sleep?
The whirlwinds wrestle and the billows rage,
And yet God holds them in his hollow palm;
He frowneth war—in conflict they engage:—
He smileth peace—and lo! there is a calm.
And oftentimes, to gaze upon the scenes,
That deck the bosom of your mother earth,
Leave the close shadows of those dark ravines
Where solitary thought alone has birth;
Leave the dense-foliaged grove and sparkling rill,
That sheds delicious coolness through your bower;
And seek the high top of some breezy hill,

And there give silent meditation power
To rule your spirit while your eyes survey
The glories spread beneath the light of day.
But, in the contemplation of such high
And glorious visions, let us not forget,
That on the splendor of the boundless sky
And on the earth, the seal of change is set!
Change is the lot of each created thing,
Change swift and constant change the seasons bring.
Mark how they change!—upon the summer's brow
Twine clustering wreaths of golden-crested grain,
The ripened fruit drops slowly from the bough,
Stirred by the gale that breathes along the plain.
Then bounteous autumn yields her liberal stores.
The tired laborer to bless and cheer,
And from her lap in glad profusion pours
Her copious gifts to crown the perfect year.
Then are the leaves all tinged with vermeil dyes,
And withering fall upon the faded grass,
And o'er the azure of the changing skies
Pale fleeting mist and drifting vapors pass.
Stern winter comes to scatter over earth
High crests of snow and jewels icy-cold;
And manhood seeks his dear, domestic hearth
Where glow affections which are never old.
Then spring, with all her bird-like melodies,

And rose-leaves twined mid her dishevelled hair,
Stirs the young foliage of the forest trees,
And with soft radiance paints the stilly air.
And there are lesser changes—Heaven is pure
To day—no scattered mists its smiles obscure—
To-morrow comes—and one continual cloud
Throws o'er the green earth an unbroken shroud—
To-day we taste the morning's dewy breath,
To-morrow brings disease and pain and death—
To-day we drink the blushing cup of health,
And see its waters sparkling soft and clear;
To-morrow comes the pestilence by stealth,
Robed in thick darkness, heralded by fear.
Even now we see the poisonous vapor sweep
Across our land, borne o'er th' extended deep;
But it may vanish soon and backward pour
To its own cave upon the Dead sea shore—
And men will lift their grateful hearts to Him,
Before whose glance the lightning's flash grows dim!
Yet, thro' such clouds of change there breaks one ray,
Whose holy light can never pass away—
It is the Word of God—here too we learn
That the free spirit will forever burn
In deathless glory, where serener skies
Bend o'er the undimmed bowers of Paradise!

And now farewell! my brothers, through my lyre
 The mournful gale is echoing farewell!
Fainter and feebler grows the poet's fire,—
 Deep as the music of a vesper-bell,
That tolls the requiem of departed day,
My last, lone, solemn strain now dies away!
My heart feels almost desolate, to think
 How, after some short hours, the two or three,
Who gather with me here upon this brink
 And narrow shoal of time, must shortly be
Forth on the sea of this unquiet world,
With sail and pennon to the breeze unfurled.
And we must separate—the little fleet
May scatter widely, never more to meet,
Except by chance upon the tossing waves;
 That hour of meeting may be calm or drear,
When the sky blushes or the tempest raves,
 But for this moment let that hour be dear.
Let us look backward to this solemn scene,
 As a clear spring upon a desert waste,
Though o'er its waters cypress branches lean,
 And though it be like Marah to the taste.
It might have been untinged with bitterness,
 Save that of parting, if from our small band
Only the absent made its numbers less;
 But on young brows hath Death's relentless hand

Impress'd his signet-ring—on lips, that glowed
  With the quick fires of sun-illumined thought,
Weighs the damp pressure of earth's icy load;
  To make her palace there, the worm has sought
The temple of a mind, which, from the sod,
Stands in the burning presence of its God!

I breathe one name, because in yonder halls
  It shed an early and a beauteous light,
As softly sweet as that which sometimes falls
  On a white temple in a silvery night.
He worshipped Learning in her ancient forms,
  And steeped his mind in farthest classic lore;
Study to him was like the sun that warms,
  And books the rays that did a lustre pour
Into his being—but his lamp grew pale;
  For he did love old knowledge better far
Than Nature's teachings—so his life did fail,
  As fails the glory of the morning star.
Goldsborough!* I knew thee but a few, brief days,
Yet knew full well thy worth above all praise.

Upon your hearts, my brothers, yet once more
  With earnest fervor would I press this truth—
That Nature has for you rich gifts in store,

* See note.

To crown the morning of unshadowed youth;
The wounds of sorrow and of guilt to cure;
To keep your early feelings fresh and pure;
And, if you read the lesson on her page
 As written there by God's all glorious hand,
Bright, in the evening of your feeble age,
 Will be your passage to the starry land.
These simple words are all my lyre can tell—
May God forever bless you, and farewell!

NOTE.

Goldsborough! I knew thee but a few brief days, &c.

Samuel Goldsborough, of Maryland, was the most distinguished classical scholar of the class of 1827. This was the first graduated class. The author was in College with him but a short time, yet long enough to appreciate his fine talents and to love his social virtue. Others of the Alumni who have died and whose memories we fondly cherish, may deserve equal commemoration with him we have mentioned; but the character of the latter proved admirably illustrative of our subject. He loved better to commune through the night watches with the spirits of ancient genius than to go forth at morning and listen to the sunrise eloquence of Nature.

www.ingramcontent.com/pod-product-compliance
Lightning Source LLC
LaVergne TN
LVHW011140110826
845150LV00008B/2428
* 9 7 8 1 4 1 8 1 9 2 6 5 5 *